GRAMMAR FOR PARENTS

GRAMMAR FOR PARENTS
How to Help Your Child
With Writing and Punctuation

Jerry George with Clare Stuart

Piccadilly Press • London

Phototypeset from author's disk by Piccadilly Press.
Printed and bound by Progressive Printing, Leigh-on-Sea
for the publishers Piccadilly Press Ltd.,
5 Castle Road, London NW1 8PR

A catalogue record for this book is available from the
British Library

ISBN: 1 85340 322 9

Jerry George lives in Canada. He is a former teacher and
headteacher and has also worked as an educational
consultant and lecturer at the University of British
Columbia.

Clare Stuart lives in Altrincham, Cheshire. She has
taught English in secondary schools for many years, and
currently teaches at Altrincham Grammar School.

CONTENTS

Introduction

INTRODUCTION

The trouble with English grammar is there seems to be so much of it. Let's face it, not many of us look forward to spending our time with a four- or five-hundred-page book with a title like "English Grammar and Usage". Yet we all recognise the importance of using "good grammar" in many situations: to create a favourable impression, to express ourselves clearly, and to improve opportunities at work.

Grammar for Parents is intended to summarise for you some of the main rules of standard written English, so that you can help your child to be a more effective writer. There may be times when you and your child will want to refer to a detailed reference book for more information, but this book offers you some basic guidelines, including:

– clear definitions of the terms we use to talk about English;
– explanations and examples of the major "rules" of English grammar;
– suggestions for using grammar creatively to improve writing;

– a "trouble-shooting" glossary of the main grammar pitfalls; those that most frequently confuse even the best of writers.

But, before you begin to help your child, here are a few points you should know about grammar:

• YOU ALREADY KNOW MORE ABOUT
GRAMMAR THAN YOU THINK YOU DO!
Grammar is the system that describes how our language works; how it is put together. It's even been described as the science of putting language in its place! It is complex, but if you speak English, you already know more English grammar than you think. For example, you would probably say,

When I see danger, I run.

You wouldn't say,

Danger run I see I when.

You already know the way in which words in English are put together into sentences. You learned it when you learned how to talk. What you may not know are the terms we use to describe this system.

• APPROPRIATE LANGUAGE DEPENDS ON THE
SITUATION
Languages such as English that are used over wide

geographical areas are divided into *dialects*, varieties of language spoken by particular groups of people. Because English is so widely used around the world, it has many varieties or dialects. For example the spoken English in London, differs from that of Toronto, Canada which in turn sounds different from the English spoken by a person in Kingston, Jamaica. There are even different dialects of English within the same country.

Children learn to speak in the dialect used in their homes and immediate environments, and their dialect is quite appropriate when talking with friends or relatives. However, often, speakers of one dialect will also understand and use the version of English that is known as standard English, and this is the dialect that is used in formal writing. It is important for children to understand the way that standard English works because this is the English that is used in institutions such as schools and universities. It is a version of English that can be understood the world over, regardless of the local dialect that may be spoken in people's homes.

• WRITTEN AND SPOKEN ENGLISH ARE DIFFERENT

Standard English gives us a common language for communicating. When we speak to another English-speaking person face-to-face, we can usually manage to communicate even if we are speaking in different dialects. This is because, if we can see each other, we can see the listener's reactions to what is being said. If he or she looks puzzled or mystified, we can repeat or rephrase what we have been saying. We can use signs and body language. We can pause or raise and lower our voices. We are more limited on the telephone, but we can still repeat and rephrase. When it comes to writing, though, we have to make our message very clear since the person reading it can't see us, or ask us any questions. Since writers don't always know who their readers will be, they have to follow rules of writing or "conventions" that everyone has agreed to try to follow.

Although we do know the grammar of our own spoken language, because this is a part of being human, your child needs to learn the conventions or agreed-upon rules of the written versions of English. These include grammar, spelling, and punctuation.

• GRAMMAR CHANGES OVER TIME TO REFLECT CHANGES IN USAGE

Languages that have been used for a long time and that have spread over the world undergo changes. New words are added and some "rules" change. For instance twenty-five years ago nobody could have told you what a "nerd" or a "dork" was.

'NERD' or 'DORK'

The rule that sentences should not end with prepositions has become more flexible over time. When Winston Churchill was admonished for reportedly saying,

"That is an outrage I will not put up with"

he corrected himself by saying,

"That is an outrage up with which I will not put".

His correction pointed out the sometimes awkward consequences of following rules that have become outmoded.

• PROFESSIONAL WRITERS SOMETIMES BREAK THE RULES OF GRAMMAR

You may have noticed in your reading, particularly of fiction, that professional writers seem to break grammar rules from time to time. Here is an example in a short excerpt from *Down with Skool* by Geoffrey Willans and Ronald Searle:

How to Avoid History

Noone hav ever found a way of avoiding history it is upon us and around us all. The only thing when you look at the cuning vilaninous faces in our class you wonder if history may not soon be worse than ever.

Do you see the run-on sentence and can you spot the spelling errors? The authors have deliberately written this as it might have been written by a schoolboy who doesn't know the rules. They are trying to create a certain effect. But remember, before your child can break the rules of grammar for effect in writing, he or she needs to know what these rules are! This little book is intended to help you understand some of these rules of written standard English, so that you can help your child be a more effective writer.

Chapter One

THE GRAMMATICAL ELEMENTS OF ENGLISH

The smallest elements to consider when looking at English grammar are individual words, sometimes called parts of speech. These combine into phrases and clauses which in turn combine to become sentences. Sentences can be of different types with different functions. The diagram on page 3 shows the various elements that make up English grammar.

TYPES OF WORDS (Parts of Speech)

Knowing the names for the function of words in sentences is mainly useful to help your child discuss writing. For example, someone might say to your child, "Try to use more adjectives", or, "It would help if you made your verbs more precise". Use the explanations which follow as references just in case your child needs them.

The first thing to know is that words become parts of speech only when they are used in sentences. The part of speech they become is determined by their use in the sentence.

Here we go.

CONTENT WORDS

These carry most of the meaning in a sentence.

NOUNS

Nouns are names and identifiers of people, places, things and ideas. They become nouns when they are used in sentences as doers or receivers of actions:

The Grammatical Elements of English

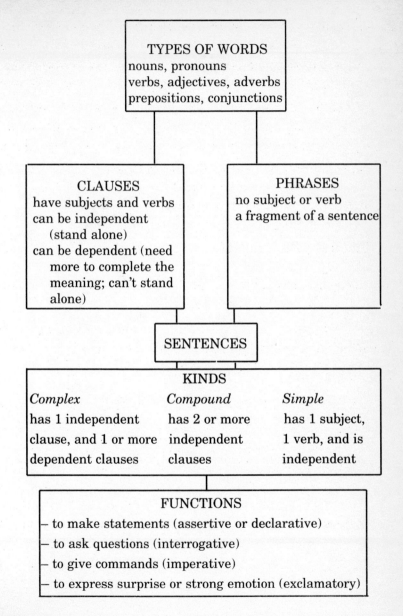

TYPES OF WORDS
nouns, pronouns
verbs, adjectives, adverbs
prepositions, conjunctions

CLAUSES
have subjects and verbs
can be independent
   (stand alone)
can be dependent (need
   more to complete the
   meaning; can't stand
   alone)

PHRASES
no subject or verb
a fragment of a sentence

SENTENCES

KINDS

Complex	*Compound*	*Simple*
has 1 independent	has 2 or more	has 1 subject,
clause, and 1 or more	independent	1 verb, and is
dependent clauses	clauses	independent

FUNCTIONS
— to make statements (assertive or declarative)
— to ask questions (interrogative)
— to give commands (imperative)
— to express surprise or strong emotion (exclamatory)

The <u>player</u> popped her <u>bubblegum</u>.
(Both words underlined are nouns – one doing the action, the other receiving it.)

An <u>adult</u> is a <u>person</u> who has stopped growing at both <u>ends</u> but not in the <u>middle</u>.
(Words underlined are nouns.)

Proper Nouns

The names of specific people, places, companies and institutions begin with capital letters. They are also known as *proper nouns*.

<u>Alistair Cooke</u> had a radio programme with the <u>British Broadcasting Corporation</u> in <u>London</u>.
<u>Martin</u> visited <u>Manchester</u> over the <u>Christmas</u> holiday.

Singular and Plural Nouns

Nouns can refer to one person, place, thing or idea, in which case they are *singular* (a *desk*, a *box*, the *computer*, a *girl*).

They can refer to more than one; in which case they are *plural* and their endings change to signal this, in most cases by adding the letters "s" or "es"(the *desks*, some *boxes*, many *computers*, fourteen *girls*).

Nouns are fairly straightforward but watch for two things:

1. Is it a proper noun needing a capital letter?
2. Is it singular or plural?

PRONOUNS

Pronouns are words used in place of nouns, often to avoid repeating the nouns.

> *Anna loves spinach. <u>She</u> really likes <u>it</u>.*

The pronoun "she" replaces the noun "Anna", and the pronoun "it" replaces the noun "spinach".

> *A cow is just a machine <u>that</u> makes grass fit for <u>us</u> to eat.*

The pronoun "that" refers to the noun "machine" and the pronoun "us" replaces the noun "people".

Your child should always make sure his or her reader knows what noun the pronoun is replacing. Here's an example where it is not clear. We are not sure who the "she" is in the second sentence.

> *Sally has a cat. <u>She</u> is very beautiful.*

Depending on the meaning intended, this would be better written,

> *Sally, who is very beautiful, has a cat.*
> or *Sally has a cat that is very beautiful.*

Pronouns, like the nouns they replace, can be subjects or objects in a sentence. Unlike nouns, some pronouns change their form when they are used as objects.

> <u>Who</u> was at the party last night? (<u>who</u> is the subject)
> <u>To whom</u> were you speaking on the phone? (<u>whom</u> is the object)

Note: "To whom" sounds very formal. In everyday speech you would be more likely to say, "Who were you speaking to on the phone?"

THE CHANGING FORMS OF PRONOUNS

PRONOUNS USED AS SUBJECTS	PRONOUNS USED AS OBJECTS
I, he, she, we, they, who, whoever	me, him, her, us, them, whom, whomever
I gave her the money.	She gave *me* the money.
He bought new running shoes.	The running shoes belong to *him*.
She heard about the contest.	Please tell *her* about the contest.
We aren't worried.	Don't worry about *us*.
They went to the office.	The teacher sent *them* to the office.

VERBS

Verbs are the action words. They make the sentence go. They allow a sentence to get somewhere. They are the words that tell what the nouns and pronouns are doing, or what is being done to them, or what they are.

> Ahmed _makes_ a living as a landscape designer. He _is_ very artistic.

> _Did_ you _hear_ the one about the mouse that _went_ to Scotland and _became_ a moose?

The bad news is there are a lot of rules for verbs. They come in tenses (present, past, future, present perfect, past perfect, and future perfect) and moods (indicative, subjunctive, imperative). The good news is your child does not have to know all the rules to be a good writer. If you suspect your child might be getting twisted up verb-wise, and asks you for help, tell him or her to trust his or her ears, read the writing out loud and see if it sounds right.

VERB TENSES

An important reminder: Make sure your child knows that it's essential to be consistent in use of tenses. When telling a story, for example, it is important not to start off in one tense, then change to another.

Present	*Past*	*Future*
I work	I worked	I shall work
I am working	I was working	I shall be working

Present Perfect	*Past Perfect*	*Future Perfect*
I have worked	I had worked	I shall have worked
I have been working	I had been working	I shall have been working

When Jamie <u>was walking</u> (past tense) *down the street, he <u>meets</u>* (present tense) *Mabel.*
When Jamie <u>was walking</u> (past tense) *down the street, he <u>met</u>* (past tense) *Mabel.*
In this short story the hero <u>becomes</u> (present tense) *lost, but then he <u>found</u>* (past tense) *his way again.*
In this short story the hero <u>becomes</u> (present tense) *lost, but then he <u>finds</u>* (present tense) *his way again.*

ADJECTIVES
Adjectives describe or tell you more about nouns and pronouns.

Arnold is a <u>mean</u>, <u>cranky</u>, <u>unpopular</u> man.

In this example the adjectives tell you more about Arnold; maybe more than you want to know.

Except for the odd spelling trap, adjectives are easy. They can help your child's writing become more interesting and precise.

ADVERBS

Adverbs describe verbs or tell you more about verbs or each other. They are used to express time, place, manner, degree and cause.

As he walked <u>slowly</u> down the dark street, the rain ceased <u>very suddenly</u>, and the moon gradually appeared in the <u>quickly</u> clearing sky.

In this example the adverbs tell you more about how he walked, how the rain ceased, and how the moon appeared and the sky cleared.

Here's another example, first, with no adverbs:

He turned and looked through the window at the leaves falling from the tree.

Then, with a few adverbs (roman):

He turned <u>slowly</u> and looked <u>indifferently</u> through the window at the leaves falling <u>softly</u> from the tree.

Your child may use adverbs in his or her writing to add colour and precision to the verbs. Adverbs answer such questions as how,when, where, how often, how long, how much?

FUNCTION WORDS

These act like the glue in a sentence, connecting or joining the content words.

CONJUNCTIONS

Conjunctions connect or link words, phrases, or clauses to each other. They are used to help join ideas together.

> Pat <u>and</u> Mike are good friends, <u>but</u> that doesn't mean they never quarrel.

Conjunctions enable your child to combine thoughts into longer sentences, and to avoid a series of short, choppy sentences.

COORDINATING CONJUNCTIONS

(connect 2 similar structures: 2 nouns, 2 phrases, 2 clauses)
and, but, or, nor, neither, yet, so, still, for.

SUBORDINATING CONJUNCTIONS

(connect clauses to the main subject and verb)
since, after, until, because, although, if, unless, where, when, while, as.

Clauses that begin with subordinating conjunctions should not be left to stand alone as though they were complete; they depend for their meaning on a main clause:

✗ *If there were no gravity.*
✓ *If there were no gravity we would fly away.*
✗ *When you take your eyes off your objective.*
✓ *You may start to see obstacles when you take your eyes off your objective.*

PREPOSITIONS

Prepositions connect or join nouns or pronouns to the rest of the sentence. They show relationships of place (*above, between, in, on, around, through, under, over*), time (*after, during, before, since, on, until*), or manner *with, like, for, of*). The noun or pronoun that follows a preposition is the object of that preposition.

> *He went to the movies; he got out at 9:30 and went into the restaurant.*

Normally you do not end a sentence with a preposition in writing since its job is to connect a noun or a pronoun with the rest of the sentence.

It isn't necessary for your child to memorise these descriptions of the parts of speech in order to write well. However, they can be useful reference points. For example, when you read your child's work you might suggest that his or her writing could be improved if nouns or adjectives were used more precisely. (*Car* is more precise than *vehicle*, and *convertible* is more precise than *car*. So the sentence,

> The <u>car</u> was parked on the street.

can be made more informative by using a more specific noun,

> The <u>convertible</u> was parked on the street.

and this in turn can be made more specific by adding adjectives,

> The <u>battered old red</u> convertible was parked on the street.

When your child is writing he or she is trying to convey meaning as completely as possible with only the printed word, and no sound or sight to help. The more precise or exact the words used the more likely the reader will get the picture.

TEST YOUR CHILD (AND YOURSELF!) ON THE
NAMES OF THE PARTS OF SPEECH

What is the type of word or part of speech of each of the words in italics?:

1. *She* was very angry and upset.
2. You can get cash *from* the banking machine.
3. You can't have your cake *and* eat it.
4. Oh, what a *beautiful* morning!
5. The actress died *dramatically*.

(*Answers: 1. pronoun 2. preposition 3. conjunction 4. adjective 5. adverb*)

SENTENCES, PHRASES AND CLAUSES

Parts of speech are grouped into phrases and clauses, which in turn make up sentences.

In this section we look at ways to identify sentences, phrases, and clauses. One of the most common traps that your child may fall into is using phrases and clauses as though they were sentences; that is, not giving enough information to the reader to make the meaning clear. In writing it is important to make sure that the reader knows to what or to whom the writer is referring.

SENTENCES

A sentence is a group of words that is sufficiently self-contained to make sense. A complete sentence has at least one subject and one verb.

Examples:

✗ *Constantly washed by water.*
✓ *A peninsula is a neck of land constantly washed by water.*
✗ *You are being inconsistent if.*
✓ *You are being inconsistent if you avoid the sun but go to a tanning salon.*
✗ *To keep flies in the house.*
✓ *Sometimes screens on windows just help to keep flies in the house.*

Functions of sentences
To make statements. *I can't yodel.*
To ask questions. *Do you like yodelling?*
To give commands. *Start to yodel at once.*
To express surprise or emotion. *You don't know how to yodel* !

Forms of sentences
A *simple* sentence has a subject and a verb. The subject is the doer of the action when the verb is active; it can be thought of as who or what the sentence is about. The verb is the word that tells about the action

the subject is doing. Every sentence has at least one subject and one verb.

John sat on the chair.

John is the subject of the sentence, doing the action; *sat* is the verb which tells what he did.

The typist prepared the report.

The *typist* is the subject; the verb is *prepared*. Who is doing the preparing? The typist!

A *complex* sentence contains a simple sentence, called an independent clause, and one or more dependent clauses beginning with a subordinating conjunction or relative pronoun.

Spring, which begins March 21, is my favourite season.

The simple sentence or independent clause is *Spring is my favourite season*. The dependent clause beginning with a relative pronoun is *which begins March 21*.

The typist was skilled, but he still made mistakes.

The simple sentence or independent clause is *The typist was skilled*. The dependent clause beginning with a subordinating conjunction is *but he still made mistakes*.

A *compound* sentence has two or more independent clauses joined by a conjunction such as the following: *or, and, but*. Each clause could stand alone as a sentence.

> *John sat on a chair and drank a cup of tea.*
> *The typist prepared the report, but his boss took all the credit.*

PHRASES

Phrases are groups of words without verbs.They are clusters of words that are not complete enough to be sentences; that is, they don't have both a subject and a verb. When verbs and other words are added to them, they can become sentences. There are several types of phrases:

Prepositional Phrases
> *to the hockey game*
> *in the backyard*
> *under the chair*
> *behind the cupboard*

These all begin with prepositions and tell you the location of something, but they cannot stand alone. They are incomplete because they don't have anything to which they refer. You don't know what or who is going to the hockey game.

Infinitive Phrases
An infinitive is part of a verb formed by putting "to" in front of it.

to run away
to jump over a hurdle

These are phrases that begin with infinitives. They cannot stand alone because they don't give enough information to make complete sense. Who is going to run away?

This is not the first time he has threatened <u>to run away</u>.
You have to be in good shape <u>to jump over a hurdle</u> like that.

Note: You will sometimes see phrases stand alone in writing. Here's an example:

"Where are you going?"
"To the hockey game"

This makes sense because the answer refers back to the question. The reader understands that the words "I am going" have been left out. Phrases only make sense in a more complete context. They provide information or description but by themselves they are incomplete. In writing, make sure your child's phrases are connected to the verbs and nouns that complete their meaning.

17

CLAUSES

CLAUSES !

Clauses have both subjects and verbs, and may contain phrases. They can be *independent*, if they can stand alone and make sense. For example,

> *I don't watch TV.*
> <u>*I don't watch TV*</u> and <u>*I don't play video games*</u>.

(Each clause is also a simple sentence. A simple sentence and an independent clause are the same thing.)

They are *dependent* (subordinate), if they need more information to be complete. For example,

> *I don't watch television programmes <u>that are violent</u>.*

The meaning of the underlined clause is not clear without the rest of the sentence to which it refers. Here's another example:

> *Gardens in Greater Manchester are hosts for huge slugs, <u>which have big appetites</u>.*

And another:

> *The girls <u>who were at the front door</u> were selling cosmetics.*

SUBORDINATE CLAUSE

QUICK REVIEW: SENTENCES, PHRASES AND CLAUSES

Sentences have verbs and subjects and can always stand alone. They have four purposes:

1. To make statements
2. To ask questions
3. To give commands
4. To express surprise or emotion

Phrases are groups of related words that can't stand alone as a sentence.

Clauses have verbs and subjects. Independent clauses can stand alone; dependent clauses cannot.

Chapter Two

PUNCTUATION

The purpose of punctuation is to allow writers to use signals as substitutes for the sounds, the pauses, and the voice tones they would use if speaking. Proper use of punctuation marks is important if you want your meaning to be clear. One of the things your child can do when he or she is writing and trying to decide what punctuation to use is to read the text aloud.

Here are some examples of some of the most used and misused punctuation marks.

THE FULL STOP

This is used to indicate the end of a sentence. A question mark (?) is also a full stop but indicates a query or some suggestion of doubt. An exclamation mark (!) indicates surprise, emotion or reader take note of this!

THE COMMA

This is the most frequently used mark within sentences. It is used:

1. to separate three or more words in a series or list but it is not usually used before "and"

I like plums, bananas, apples and pears.
The dreariest winter months are December,
January, February and March.

2. to set off a phrase that explains the noun it follows

I was talking about Anne, the doctor.

3. to separate phrases or dependent clauses that add information but aren't essential to the meaning

He was too young for the war, which took place
between 1939 and 1945.

4. to set off dates, places, and persons' names

He was born on February 21, 1977, in Altrincham,
Cheshire.
You, Katie, are a very understanding person.

5. whenever needed to avoid possible confusion

To win Henrietta, Thomas will have to try to be
more pleasant.

or

To win, Henrietta Thomas will have to try to be
more pleasant.

Commas have many possible uses within sentences, and the potential for misusing them is correspondingly great. If your child is unsure about inserting a comma suggest that he or she tries reading the sentence aloud. If a pause seems natural, then a comma should be used!

THE COLON
The colon is most often used to introduce a list or a long quotation.

✓ *English is spoken in: Australia, New Zealand, and the United States of America.*
✓ *English is spoken in the following countries: Australia, New Zealand and the United States of America.*

Joseph Conrad begins his novel by describing his main character: he was an inch, perhaps two, under six feet, powerfully built, and he advanced straight at you with a slight stoop of the shoulders, head forward, and a fixed from-under stare which made you think of a charging bull.
   (Lord Jim)

THE SEMI-COLON
This punctuation mark is used when you want to stress a close connection between two independent clauses in a sentence. It is most often used when the second clause begins with one of the following words: *consequently, hence, however, so, yet, furthermore, otherwise, then, namely, for example, nevertheless, therefore, for instance, that is.*

23

I'm sorry I won't be there; otherwise I'd gladly help.
He is a very boring person; for example he talks
about himself all the time.

QUOTATION MARKS

These are used when you are writing the exact words
of a speaker, or when you want to isolate a specific
word or group of words.

The salesperson said, "We have a special deal on
this particular item."
The poet W.H. Auden once said, "A professor is one
who talks in someone else's sleep."
The word "awful" once meant full of awe.

THE APOSTROPHE

This punctuation mark is often misused, although the
rules for its use are simple.

1. It can indicate possession, in which case add it
before the letter "s". In most cases this indicates possession by just one person.

Lynn's car
life's problems
the judge's decision
the teacher's notes.

If the word already ends in "s", you can just add the
apostrophe. In most cases, this indicates possession

by more than one person.

the Browns' house

If the word already ends in "s" and is singular, then an apostrophe and then the letter "s" can be added,

Charles's elephant.

An exception to this is the word "its" which does not have an apostrophe to indicate possession. Do not use an apostrophe with the possessive pronouns yours, his, hers, theirs, ours.

2. The apostrophe has a second important function. Use it to replace a letter or letters that have been left out of a word.

You're a very clever person. (you are)
It's going to rain. (it is)

3. Finally, use an apostrophe when writing the plurals of numerals and letters.

How many s's are in Mississippi? How many 6's in 36?

PARENTHESES AND DASHES

Like commas, parentheses (or brackets) and dashes are used to mark pauses in sentences. Parentheses allow you to add information some people may not know.

Michael J. Fox (the Canadian actor) is making a new film.
My cousin (the younger one) is visiting this weekend.

Use the dash for sudden or abrupt interruptions.

If you want to make friends, you should often – even always – be pleasant.
That was an odd – no, a really stupid – thing to do.

ELLIPSES ...

Ellipses are used in quotations to show where words have been left out. For example, here is a statement you might wish to shorten:

William Shakespeare, who lived in the sixteenth century, wrote many plays for the theatre, including comedies, tragedies and histories.

Use ellipses to show where words have been left out.

William Shakespeare ... wrote ... comedies, tragedies and histories.

QUICK REVIEW: PUNCTUATION

Basically, you use the following punctuation marks:

a full stop (.) at the end of a sentence to signal its completion

a comma (,) to indicate a shorter pause

a colon (:) at the beginning of a list introduced by a complete sentence.

a semi-colon (;) instead of a full stop between closely related sentences

a question mark (?) after a question

an exclamation mark (!) to express surprise or emotion

quotation marks (" ") to signal exact words spoken

apostrophe (') for possession or in place of letters left out of a word

parentheses ( ) to add information some readers may need

ellipses (...) to show where words have been left out of a quotation

a dash (–) as an alternative to a comma, to express emphasis

Chapter Three

USING GRAMMAR TO IMPROVE WRITING

Good writing isn't just a matter of avoiding mistakes. There are many positive steps your child can take to make his or her writing more vigorous, interesting and appealing. You want to be sure your child's ideas are communicated as effectively as possible, and this is where skill in using appropriate grammatical structures will be helpful.

REVISION: COMMUNICATING THE CONTENT EFFECTIVELY

When your child begins to write, the most important thing is to get thoughts down, even in point form. There is no need to worry too much at this stage about grammar or spelling. Much of what your child writes, however, may have to be revised and edited before anyone else reads it.

What's the difference between revising and editing?

Revision is the process of "seeing again", and reworking to improve the clarity of ideas. There are basically four things your child can do to make certain he or she is communicating the content effectively:

1.*add*
2.*take away*
3.*re-order*, or
4. *substitute / change*

a word, a phrase, a sentence, a paragraph, or a whole section.

The following passage could be changed in a variety of ways:

As soon as the snow melts, many people like to spend more time outdoors. They might be gardeners, anxious to begin working in the soil. Perhaps, on the other hand, they enjoy cycling and with milder weather they can pursue this outdoor pastime.

1. Your child could *add* words.

As soon as the snow melts, many <u>active</u> people like to spend much more time <u>in the great</u> outdoors. They might be <u>avid</u> gardeners, anxious to begin working in the soil. Perhaps, on the other hand, they enjoy cycling and with <u>the newly arrived</u> milder weather they can pursue this <u>envigorating</u> outdoor pastime.

2. Your child could take *away words* and phrases.

> *As soon as the snow melts,...people ... spend more time outdoors. They might be gardeners, anxious to begin working. ... Perhaps ... they enjoy cycling and ... can pursue this ... pastime.*

3. Your child could *re-order* the passage.

> *Many people like to spend more time outdoors as soon as the snow melts. They might enjoy cycling, and with milder weather, they can pursue this outdoor pastime. On the other hand, they might be gardeners, anxious to begin working in the soil.*

4. Your child could *substitute / change* words or phrases.

> *When the snow is gone, most people like to spend more time outside. They might enjoy playing football or cricket. On the other hand, they might be golfers, anxious to get out on the course.*

TIPS FOR COMPOSING AND REVISING

1. CONSIDER THE AUDIENCE.

When your child is writing quite informally, as in a personal letter, he or she will want to consider writing more than one draft. If so, the first draft could even be in note form. When writing for an outside audience, your child will have to make decisions about the style to adopt. Who will read the writing – a friend, a teacher, a seven-year-old, someone living in another country, a girlfriend's father, a boyfriend's mother, a prospective employer? He or she should try to imagine the reader and adjust the writing accordingly. Should the style be formal or informal?

2. AVOID "OVER-WRITING".

'I HEREBY PROCLAIM, MRS STIGGINS, THAT I WOULD BE UNQUESTIONABLY DELIGHTED TO PARTAKE OF LUNCHEON WITH YOUR GOOD SELF AND YOUR DEAR SON, STEVE, ON SUNDAY...'

AVOID 'OVER-WRITING'

Always try to eliminate unnecessary words. This will help your child be more precise, and will make the writing more direct and easier to read. For example,

In order to understand this idea, it is necessary to be constantly working and studying.

This could be shortened to

Studying will help you understand this idea.

3. USE THE ACTIVE RATHER THAN THE PASSIVE VOICE.
The verb is in the active voice when the subject does the action.

I <u>type</u> my own letters. (active)
Henrietta <u>drove</u> her car to the garage. (active)
The artist <u>painted</u> a beautiful picture. (active)

The verb is in the passive voice when the subject receives the action.

My letters <u>are typed</u> by me. (passive)
Her car <u>was driven</u> by Henrietta to the garage. (passive)
A beautiful picture <u>was painted</u> by the artist. (passive)

The active voice is more direct and doesn't take as many words as the passive. Generally speaking, your child should have the subjects of the sentences *do* rather than *receive* actions.

Phyllis <u>was given</u> a new car by her father for her graduation could be changed to

Phyllis's father <u>gave</u> her a new car for her graduation.

Similarly, your child should avoid overuse of the verb "to be", and should use strong verbs to improve the prose. When the verb "to be" is followed by a noun that also has a verb form, generally speaking he or she should use that verb form rather than "to be" with a noun. Here are some examples:

Noun	*Verb*
drinker	drink
painter	paint
farmer	farm

He is a frequent <u>drinker</u> of milk

could be changed to

He frequently <u>drinks</u> milk.

Claude Monet was a landscape painter

could be changed to

Claude Monet <u>painted</u> landscapes.

In the Middle Ages peasants were <u>farmers</u> for the nobility

could be changed to

In the Middle Ages peasants <u>farmed</u> for the nobility.

4. USE PARALLEL STRUCTURE.

In a series or list, your child should begin each item in the list with the same part of speech.

If your child's list is nouns, use only nouns. For example,

> *For this exercise you will need paper, pencil, pen and an eraser*
> *For this exercise you will need paper, pencil, pen, and to erase.*

In the following list, all the items begin with the same part of speech, the infinitive form of the verb.

> *Some of the purposes of writing are:*
> *– to allow us to communicate with others*
> *– to help us clarify what we know about a topic*
> *– to let us use our imaginations*

not

> *Some of the purposes of writing are:*
> *– to allow us to communicate with others*
> *– helping us to clarify what we know about a topic*
> *– to let us use our imagination*

5. COMBINE SHORT SENTENCES.

Your child should use sentence-combining when he or she has a series of short, choppy sentences. Try reading aloud to hear if the writing has too many full stops.

Bill has skis. They are new. They have the latest bindings.

These three short sentences could be combined.

Bill has new skis with the latest bindings.

Here's another:

Ahmed works every day at the restaurant.
He works after school.

These two sentences could be combined to read

Ahmed works at the restaurant every day after school.

Sometimes two independent clauses can be combined by making one of them subordinate.

The meeting was postponed.
The subject of the meeting was procrastination.

Combined:

The meeting, <u>which was on procrastination</u>, was postponed.

These same two clauses could be combined by changing one of them to a phrase.

The meeting about procrastination was postponed.

Ideas expressed in clauses or phrases can often be written as single words. For example,

The person who is brilliant will surely succeed.

can be expressed

The brilliant person will surely succeed.

And

The house constructed of brick was situated on a hillside.

can become

The brick house was situated on a hillside.

Children can become more aware of the effects of sentence-combining if they spend a little time on de-combining sentences. This involves reducing longer sentences to shorter ones, sometimes reconstructing them in alternate ways for different effects.

For example, here is a sentence with several combined ideas:

The fog rolled in from the inlet on a vast front, enveloping first the shore line and then, one after another, all the houses on the hill.

It could be de-combined as follows:

The fog rolled in.
It came from the inlet.
It came on a vast front.
It enveloped the shore line first.
It enveloped all the houses.
It enveloped them one after another.
The houses were on the hill.

These single ideas could be re-combined in a different way.

All the hillside houses were enveloped one after another.

To appreciate a writer's style and to get a sense of how words and phrases can be manipulated for different effects, you might now and then select a passage from a text and "play" with it. You could de-combine the passage, then experiment with re-combining by using adjectives, adverbs, phrases and clauses.

6. ORGANISE PARAGRAPHS.
There are few precise rules for paragraphing. Generally, sentences that deal with the same topic are put into one paragraph. When you change topics, start a new paragraph. Sometimes you can use connecting words or phrases to signal a new paragraph (secondly, on the other hand, alternatively, additionally, etc).

Paragraphs usually have one sentence, called the topic sentence, that tells what the paragraph is about.

The topic sentence is supported by other sentences that give more details or examples. The topic sentence most often occurs at the beginning, and sometimes at the end of the paragraph.

If your child is writing dialogue, he or she should change paragraphs every time the speaker changes, even if the speaker says only one word and the paragraph is very short.

"Are you planning to take any holidays?" asked Bill.
"Yes," replied Matt.

Although paragraphs can be written in block form, with no indentation, it is often useful to indent to signal to your reader that you are changing topic. The next paragraph is indented to show what this looks like.

Try organising your writing under headings. Ask what one or two words would give the main idea of what this part is about. These headings will allow you to "chunk" your writing into paragraphs, and will give you a start for writing topic sentences.

7. ORGANISE INFORMATION.

There are two major kinds of writing your child may be required to do. The first is narrative or story, which is made up in much the same way as anecdotes, short stories, and novels. The second type of writing is called exposition. This type of writing is used when your child has to organise and present information or explain something.

Richard Saul Wurman in his book *Information Anxiety* points out that there are five ways of organising information: category, time, location, alphabet, and continuum. When your child writes exposition, explanation, or information, he or she should try using one or more of these frameworks.

For example, suppose your child has been given or has decided on a very broad topic such as "sports". Where can he or she begin?

a. *organising by category*
What categories could the broad topic of "sports" be divided into? Contrasting categories such as the following could be used:

individual vs. team sports
professional vs. amateur sports
indoor vs. outdoor sports
sports requiring little or no equipment vs. sports needing much equipment
spectator sports vs. participatory sports

Then for each of these contrasting categories your child would list examples. These examples would in turn give an outline for the essay, and topics for the paragraphs.

b. organising by time

Using this method, your child might discuss the earliest sports, then lead up to popular modern sports.

- What kinds of sports were played in the ancient world? by the Greeks? the Romans? Africans? Chinese?
- What sports were popular in the Middle Ages? Where?
- What are currently popular sports? Where?

c. organising on a continuum

- from most physically demanding to least demanding
- from most expensive to least expensive
- from most to least dangerous.

Some of these categories can overlap, but choosing one does give your child a pattern he or she can follow when writing, and this in turn helps to paragraph appropriately.

How easy would it be for your child to write on these topics, using one of the organisational patterns? Try it and see!

shoes
trees
hats
board games
cars
transportation

8. CONSIDER USING FIGURATIVE LANGUAGE

Depending on their purpose, writers often use imagery or figurative language to convey their meanings more fully. Consider the following:

- *imagery*: Images, or mental pictures of colour and sound help to set the mood of a piece of writing. For example, words such as "darkness", "gloom" and "shadows" create one kind of mood; words such as "sunny", "bright", or "chirping" create a more cheery scene.

- *metaphors and similes*: Writers often use comparisons called metaphors or similes. Metaphors are direct comparisons of two unlike things that have one or more things in common. For example,

   Murdoch is a fox
(meaning he has some of the characteristics of a fox).
   That car is a rocket.

Similes are comparisons that use the word "like" or "as".

   He is as tall as a lamp post.

Both similes and metaphors are so much a part of everyday language that they can quickly become cliches. For example, the following phrases are likely to sound very familiar:

bright as a button
quick as a flash
bold as brass

Good writers try to avoid cliches and find fresh comparisons to get their ideas across. Ask your child how he or she could change the above overused comparisons.

bright as (a butterfly? a good idea? a ray of hope?)
quick as (a tax collector?)
bold as (a billionaire? a magpie?)

• *symbols*: In literature, symbols are concrete objects that represent or stand for something else, often an idea or feeling. For example, a snake has been used to represent evil, a dove often stands for peace, a red rose for love.

• *personification*: This is another type of comparison, in which the writer gives human characteristics to non-human things or ideas. For example,

The sun smiled brightly.
The clouds glowered menacingly.
The wind sang softly.

• *alliteration*: This device, often used in poetry, makes language appeal to our ears. Consonant sounds at the beginning of words are repeated in successive words. For example,

Slowly, silently the snake skulked ...

Whether or not your child tries some of the above techniques will depend on the purpose and audience for writing. They might not be appropriate in a business letter, for example, or an information report. However, he or she might want to try them in more imaginative or creative writing.

CHECKLIST FOR REVISION

Before editing for grammar, punctuation and spelling, your child should have another look at his or her writing to see if it can be improved. Sometimes it is helpful for a parent to do this with a child in order to look at the writing with "fresh eyes."

Consider the following points in any revision and ask your child if he or she can:

	Yes	No

1. eliminate any unnecessary words, phrases, or sentences.
2. add some words, phrases, or sentences to make your meaning really clear.
3. change the order of any of the ideas.
4. use a thesaurus or a dictionary to find better words to express something.
5. combine any sentences into longer sentences.
6. consider also whether the style is appropriate for the audience.
7. check for any violations of parallel structure.
8. consider whether comparisons would make the writing more interesting or effective.
9. do anything else to improve his or her writing style.

Chapter Four

AVOIDING COMMON GRAMMAR TRAPS

Once your child has revised his or her writing for content and organisation, the work should be edited. This process involves checking grammar, punctuation and spelling by reference to conventions. Here are some of the most common problems with grammar that writers have.

SUBJECT-VERB AGREEMENT
Rule: *Nouns and verbs must agree in number.*
What's wrong with these sentences?:

He go to the back yard.
They loves to eat.
Cats doesn't like water.

It should be obvious to your child that they don't sound right! The reason they don't sound right is that the subjects do not agree in number with their verbs.

He is singular and requires a singular form of the verb, *goes*.

They is plural and requires a plural form of the verb, *love*.

Cats is also plural, and requires a plural form of the verb, *don't*.

SUBJECT-VERB AGREEMENT : NOUNS AND VERBS MUST AGREE IN NUMBER

It is trickier to notice subject-verb disagreement when a group of words comes between the subject and the verb, as in

The hen with all her little chickens cross the road.

This should be

The hen with all her little chickens <u>crosses</u> the road.

The rule is to find the subject or doer of the action, and make it agree in number with the verb.

Here are a few more rules for subject-verb agreement that your child should be aware of:

1. When you use "there" with the verb "to be", use the singular form "is" or "was" when the noun following is singular.

> *There is a fly in my soup.*
> *There was one person who didn't arrive on time.*

Use the plural form "are" or "were" when the noun following is plural:

> *There are more ways to do this than I realised.*
> *There were a hundred and one dalmatians.*

2. Generally, use a plural verb with two subjects joined by "and".

> *Lee and Jeff are friends.*

When you connect two subjects using "both" and "and", the verb is plural:

> *Both Lee and Jeff were at the game.*

(Exceptions are "bacon and eggs", "rock and roll", and similar expressions that are considered to be singular because they refer to one concept.)

3. Use a singular verb with singular pronoun subjects such as the following:

everybody, somebody, nobody, no one, anyone, either, neither

✓ <u>*Nobody wants*</u> *the job.*
✗ <u>*Nobody want*</u> *the job.*
✓ <u>*Neither*</u> *of these movies* <u>*is*</u> *playing at the Rialto.*
✗ <u>*Neither*</u> *of these movies* <u>*are*</u> *playing at the Rialto.*

PRONOUN FORMS

1. When your child becomes a good writer he or she will know that a pronoun must agree with its antecedent in number. (An antecedent is the word that the pronoun stands for or refers to.)

> <u>*Miru*</u> *raised* <u>*her*</u> *voice.*
> *The* <u>*people*</u> *cheered* <u>*their*</u> *hero.*

In the above sentences, the singular pronoun "her" agrees with its singular antecedent "Miru". The plural pronoun "their" agrees with its plural antecedent.

The following words are singular, and generally should be followed by another singular pronoun form:

everybody, somebody, nobody, someone, everyone, no one, anyone, either, neither.

> *Neither* of the girls *has* her lunch.
> *Everyone* expressed *his* or *her* opinion.

However, when they are speaking informally, people often use the plural pronoun form. For example,

> *Everyone likes to have their own way.*
> *Someone broke into the house and they stole a TV set.*

Some authorities now suggest that when you are making a general statement, and you do not know the sex of the person, you can use "their" or "they" to avoid the awkward use of "his" and "her".

✓ *Nobody goes to a symphony concert unless he or she has a bad cough.*
✓ *Nobody goes to a symphony concert unless they have a bad cough.*
✓ *Everyone who crosses a street takes his or her life in his or her hands.*
✓ *Everyone who crosses a street takes their life in their hands.*

This is an example of a rule of grammar that is changing with common usage.

2. Most pronouns change form depending on whether they are subjects or objects in the sentence.

Here is an example that often causes problems for writers:

✓ *To <u>whom</u> were you speaking. (<u>whom</u> is the object of the preposition <u>to</u>)*
✗ *To <u>who</u> were you speaking? or Who were you speaking to?*

Remember that variations in usage are generally considered inappropriate in more formal written English, although they are quite common in spoken English.

Be careful to use the correct pronoun form in compound subjects and objects.

✓ *They invited Kim and <u>me</u> to the party.* (object)
✗ *They invited Kim and <u>I</u> to the party.*
✓ *Between you and <u>me</u>, I thought the film was dull.* (object)
✗ *Between you and <u>I</u>, I thought the party was dull.*

One way for your child to avoid confusion and test whether what he or she is writing sounds right, is to leave out the first part of the compound object. You wouldn't say,
     They invited ... I to the party.

3. When using pronouns always make sure the reader will know to whom the pronoun is referring.

Henry told his best friend that <u>he</u> would have no difficulty.

Does "he" refer to Henry or to Henry's friend? Better to reword this sentence so that there is no possibility of misunderstanding.

You could rewrite it like this:

Henry told his best friend, "I will have no difficulty."
or,
Henry told his best friend, "You will have no difficulty."
or even,
Henry told his best friend that he, Henry, would have no difficulty.

Here's another example of a confused reference:
I finally finished that book on the American Civil War, <u>which</u> was very long.

Was it a long war or a long book or both?
How would you resolve this? You could write,

I finally finished that long book on the American Civil War.

When in doubt, reword the sentence.

THE COMMA SPLICE AND THE RUN-ON SENTENCE

A comma splice occurs when a writer uses a comma instead of a full stop or semi-colon to separate two sentences.

All the schools were closed, there was a big blizzard.

This error can be corrected as follows:

> *All the schools were closed. There was a big blizzard*

or,

> *All the schools were closed; there was a big blizzard*

or even,

> *All the schools were closed because there was a big blizzard.*

A *run-on sentence* occurs when the writer forgets to use necessary punctuation between clauses or sentences. This may result in ambiguity or just plain nonsense!

> *All the schools were closed there was a big blizzard. King Charles walked and talked half an hour after his head was cut off.*

The best way for your child to spot these errors is to read the sentences aloud exactly as they have been written, or ask you to read them aloud as they listen. Do they make sense? Are they clear? If your child has any doubts then he or she must think again. What is the problem? How can it be resolved?

SENTENCE FRAGMENTS

Sentence fragments are actually phrases or clauses trying to pass as sentences. Generally, they are missing a subject or a verb. Fragments can usually be recognised by isolating them from the rest of the text to see if they can stand alone and make sense. We often speak in sentence fragments, because our listeners have more context to help get the meaning. When we write, however, we must supply all the context. Here are some examples of sentence fragments:

the snarling dog
all the time
flying through the air
which was no more than I expected.

Each of these lacks a context and is incomplete because either a subject or a verb is missing. Your child must supply more information, either by putting each in a sentence or by giving each a context so that the meaning is clear. The first one, for instance, could be changed to,

I was very much afraid of the snarling dog.
or even,
What was I afraid of? The snarling dog.

COMPARATIVE AND SUPERLATIVE (Adjectives and Adverbs)
When two people or things are compared the comparative form is used.

Mabel is <u>brighter</u> than I am in the morning.
The sun is <u>hotter</u> than any planet.
The game was <u>more</u> hotly contested than we expected.

The comparative of short words is formed by adding er to the word. The comparative form of longer adjectives or adverbs is formed by adding the word "more" before the word.

This route is <u>more</u> interesting than the other.
Bears are <u>more</u> dangerous when they have cubs.
Deer can run <u>more</u> quickly than humans.

The *superlative* form is used when *three* or more people or things are compared. It is formed by adding *est* to shorter words, or putting *most* before longer words.

He is the <u>slowest</u> person in the class.
She won the race because she was <u>most quickly</u> off the mark.

When errors are made it is often because the superlative is used when there are only two things or people being compared. For example,

✗ *Morgan is the best of the two brothers at singing.*

should be corrected to read

✓ *Morgan is the better of the two brothers at singing.*

Since the superlative is used as the highest degree of comparison it should not be qualified by words like "most" or "very". For example, in the sentence

Brian has very unique qualifications.

the word "unique" means at the top, completely individual; the word "very" should not be added. The words "very" or "most" should not be added to any words that are already in the superlative, such as the following:

best, worst, farthest, brightest, highest.

REDUNDANCY OR UNNECESSARY REPETITION

Sometimes writers qualify words unnecessarily. For example, you may have seen the expression "free gift" used in advertisements. A "gift" means something that is free. The term doesn't need to be qualified by repeating the word free. If it's not free, it's not a gift!

Here's another example:

They decided to pay their taxes in annual yearly installments.

The word "annual" already means yearly, and so both terms are not needed.

Look again at the heading for this section. What do you notice?

CONFUSING HOMOPHONES

Homophones are words that sound the same, but have different meanings. Some of these are high frequency words, and their different meanings should be kept in mind. For example,

their, they're and there.

The first one, *their*, is a possessive adjective and should be used to modify nouns or pronouns.

They admitted that it was <u>their</u> own fault.
They put on <u>their</u> uniforms to go to the ceremony.

The second one, *they're*, is the short form for they are.

I think <u>they're</u> the best people to do the job.
<u>They're</u> coming over around nine.

The third one, *there*, is an adverb of place.

Put it over <u>there</u>, please.
It was <u>there</u> the last time I looked.

DOUBLE NEGATIVES

Do not use more than one negative word to express a negative thought. For example, there are two negative words (n't, and no) in.

He <u>hasn't</u> got <u>no</u> money

Instead, write either,

He <u>hasn't any</u> money.
or
He <u>has no</u> money.

Here are some more examples of double negatives; all of them can be fixed by dropping one of the negatives and keeping the other:

Alfred <u>didn't</u> do <u>nothing</u>.
We <u>weren't</u> going <u>nowhere</u>.
<u>Nobody</u> is <u>not</u> coming with us.

CHECKLIST FOR EDITING GRAMMAR

After your child has revised his or her writing, it should be edited for possible grammatical errors. It is sometimes very helpful to share the editing with you. You can read it aloud as your child listens, and then you can both discuss ways to improve or clarify the writing.

Grammatical Point

1. Do the subjects agree in number with their verbs?
2. Are the pronoun antecedents clear?
3. Are there any comma splices or run-on sentences?
4. Are there any sentence fragments?
5. Are the comparatives and superlatives used correctly?
6. Are there any redundant expressions?
7. Are there any misspellings?
8. Are there any other grammatical points you are uncertain about?

Questions and Additional Comments:

Edited by (child)   (parent)
       Name   Name

Date:

Chapter Five

TIPS ON SPELLING

There is scarcely anyone who does not hesitate, at one time or another, over the spelling of a word. Yet most of us spell correctly most of the time. The words that give trouble are relatively few in number. In fact, here is a list of the 25 most frequently misspelled words:

again	didn't	know	something	upon
another	friend	let's	that's	went
beautiful	heard	off	their	were
because	into	our	there	when
caught	it's	said	they	where

These are high usage words and give trouble for a number of reasons. One may be that some of them are homophones. They sound the same as other words (their, there, they're; where, we're). Here's a little poem which will show your child how far people can go wrong because of English homophones. It's also a warning not to trust a computer's spelling checker too far! Try reading it aloud.

KNOW MORE MISS STEAKS
I have a spelling checker
It came with my PC
It planely marks for my revue
Mistakes I cannot sea.
I've run this poem threw it
I'm sure your please to no.
It's letter perfect in its weigh
My checker tolled me sew.

(Stephen Hume, *The Vancouver Sun*, 21/06/93)

Four of the 25 words in the list use the apostrophe to indicate that a letter has been omitted didn't, let's, that's, it's. The best way for your child to learn to spell these and other words is not to memorise the rules but to memorise the words themselves. Here's how to do it:

LOOK at the word carefully
SAY it aloud softly
WRITE the word
CHECK to see if what your child has written is correct
REPEAT the procedure if necessary.

MORE TIPS FOR SPELLING CORRECTLY

Your child may find some of the following tips helpful:

1. LEARN TO PRONOUNCE THE WORDS
CORRECTLY.
Some words create problems because they are often mispronounced:

February, not Febuary
Wednesday, not Wensday
pronunciation, not pronounciation
accidentally, not accidently
could've, not could of
might've, not might of

2. RECOGNISE COMMON SPELLING PATTERNS.
There are certain spelling patterns some people find helpful to remember:

use "i" before "e" except after "c"
deceive, receive, achieve, chief, belief

and when sounded like 'a'
  neigh, neighbour, reign, sleigh

adding prefixes does not change the word's spelling
  natural   *<u>un</u>natural*
  mobile   *<u>im</u>mobile*
  run   *<u>over</u>run*

when a word ends in a vowel, adding suffixes often doesn't change the spelling
  hope
  hope<u>ful</u>
  courage
  courage<u>ous</u>

but when a word ends in a consonant, the consonant is often doubled when adding -ing or -ed
  run   *run<u>n</u>ing*
  drop   *drop<u>p</u>ing*
  label   *label<u>l</u>ed*

There are rules and exceptions for suffixes, and it's best just to learn the most frequently used words:
  dine, dining not *dinning*;
  sun, sunny not *suny*;
  hope, hoping not *hopping*

3. TRY USING A MNEMONIC DEVICE.
Some people like to use what are called mnemonic devices as an aid to memorising the words which they

never seem able to remember. Here are some examples:

A friend is a friend to the end
(to remember that the word friend" ends with "end')';

One cap and two socks
(to remember that "necessary" has one "c" and two "s's").

Dessert has two s's, because you always want two of them
(to remember the difference between "dessert" and "desert")

The vegetable is on the table
to remember that "vegetable" ends in "table."

You could help your child to make up his or her own for those really tricky words.

In the end, the best rule to follow is

Instead of your child trying to learn the rules and their exceptions, he or she should learn to spell the words themselves. A personal list should be kept of words your child is trying to learn how to spell, and as they are mastered they should be in a special "victory" column. Your child should group the words that seem to fall into the same categories, such as enough and tough. (In each the "ough" is spelled the same and sounds the same.)

Chapter Six

SORTING OUT CONFUSING WORDS

Even the best of writers at times forget how to use some of the words in this list. They are arranged here alphabetically for quick reference.

AMOUNT/NUMBER
Use *number* for countable items; *amount* for uncountables.

> *The <u>number</u> of bikes . . .*
> *The <u>amount</u> of time . . .*

ACCEPT/EXCEPT/EXPECT
Accept means to receive or approve. *Except* means excluding. *Expect* means to think likely.

> *I <u>accept</u> your kind offer of a ride home, <u>except</u> I won't be able to leave for twenty minutes because I <u>expect</u> that I'll have to lock up everywhere.*

AFFECT/EFFECT
Affect is a verb, meaning to change. *Effect* is a noun.

He is not <u>affected</u> by heights. I, on the other hand feel the <u>effect</u> if I am on the first rung of a ladder.

ALREADY/ALL READY
Already means before this time; *all ready* means completely ready.

If everybody is <u>all ready</u> we can get going because the rest have gone <u>already</u>.

ALTOGETHER/ALL TOGETHER
Altogether means completely. *All together* means as a group.

If we don't forget the words <u>altogether</u>, and we manage to start singing at the same time, we should be able to finish <u>all together</u>.

AMONG/BETWEEN
Use *between* two; *among* three or more.

There are twenty-four sweets to share <u>among</u> four people, which means you and I can have six <u>between</u> us.

BEAR/BARE
A *bear* is an animal (noun); *bare* is without cover (adjective).

Don't ever try to tackle a <u>bear</u> with your <u>bare</u> hands.

BERTH/BIRTH

A *berth* is a narrow bed on a train or ship; *birth* refers to being born or at the beginning.

I prefer a lower <u>berth</u> on the train.
A new <u>birth</u> in the family is welcome news.

BRAKE/BREAK

A *brake* is an instrument for slowing or stopping a machine (noun);*break* is to open up or come apart.

Apply your <u>brakes</u> carefully on slippery roads. Be careful not to <u>break</u> that glass.

CAN/MAY

Can indicates ability to; *may* indicates permission.

You <u>can</u> enter a licensed establishment when you are under the legal age. You <u>may</u> not, however, purchase any alcoholic beverage.

CITE/SITE

Cite means to mention verb; a *site* is a place or location (noun).

I can <u>cite </u>several examples of historical blunders. This building is on a beautiful <u>site</u>.

CLOTH/CLOTHES

A *cloth* is a piece of fabric; *clothes* are garments for the body.

How many dish <u>cloths</u> are in the laundry basket?
She always wears very fashionable <u>clothes</u>.

COARSE/COURSE
Coarse can mean rough or vulgar; *course* can mean direction or a series of studies.

I find most heavy woollen sweaters too <u>coarse</u>.
He said he would enroll in another <u>course</u>.
Nature will run its <u>course</u>.

DESERT/DESSERT
Desert (noun) is land, usually hot and dry. *Desert* (verb) is to leave or abandon. *Dessert* (noun) is eaten after a main course.

The <u>desert</u> is hot in daytime but cold at night.
To <u>desert</u> from the army in war time is a serious offence.
The <u>dessert</u> consisted of berries and ice cream.

DISSENT/DESCENT
Dissent is to differ, to have another opinion. A *descent* goes from a higher to a lower place.

One senator decided to <u>dissent</u> from the majority.
The <u>descent</u> into the valley was very steep.

ETC.
Etc. means and so on. It is usually set off by a comma.

I have to clean my room, study, <u>etc</u>.

FEWER/LESS
Fewer is used with countable numbers; *less* with "uncountables".

*There were <u>fewer</u> people at the concert than
expected.*
It is usually <u>less</u> costly to do simple repairs yourself.

FORMERLY/FORMALLY
Formerly means previously or at a time before; *formally* means according to the rules.

I was <u>formerly</u> employed by that company.
We have never been <u>formally</u> introduced.

FORTH/FOURTH
Forth means onward or forward; *fourth* is a rank after third.

They went <u>forth</u> bravely to do battle.
She was <u>fourth</u> in the high jump event.

GOOD/WELL
Good is used as an adjective; *well* as an adverb.

He was a <u>good</u> prospect in the minor leagues.
*When he was promoted to the first division, he did
<u>well</u>.*

HOPEFULLY
Often used incorrectly to mean "I hope", the precise meaning is "in a hopeful manner."

✗ _Hopefully, the weather will be good for the picnic._
✓ _He waited hopefully for the letter._

I MYSELF
I _myself_ (or I personally. . .) is redundant. Generally, it's best to use "I" by itself.

✗ _I myself think_ . . .
✓ _I think_ . . .

IF I WAS/WERE
Use _were_ after "if" only when discussing an imaginary or hypothetical situation.

I don't know if he was there or not.
If I were prime minister, things would be different.

ITS/IT'S
Its is a possessive pronoun and has no apostrophe. _It's_ is a contraction meaning it is or it has.

The cat was asleep in its basket.
It's nice to see an animal at rest.
It's been a terrible day.

LIE/LAY
Lie means to recline; *lay* means to place or is used as
the past tense of lie.

> *Why don't you <u>lie</u> down?*
> *He <u>lay</u> down for a nap yesterday.*
> *Would you <u>lay</u> the book on the table, please?*

LIKE/AS IF
Like is used to compare two things. In formal writing,
it is not substituted for "*as if*".

> *He eats <u>like</u> a horse.*
> *It looks <u>as if</u> it's going to rain tonight.*

LOSE/LOOSE
Lose is to misplace; *loose* is unrestricted or unhin-
dered.

> *Try not to <u>lose</u> money at the race track.*
> *I prefer to wear <u>loose</u> shirts.*

ME/I
Me is used as an object; *I* as a subject.

> *Just between you and <u>me</u>, <u>I</u> prefer to stay home.*

MORAL/MORALE
Moral is having to do with right or wrong noun or
adjective; *morale* means confidence noun.

*People who want to lead the country should have
high <u>moral</u> character.*
The team's <u>morale</u> was low when they lost.

MINER/MINOR
A *miner* (noun) is one who works in a mine; *minor*
(adjective) means small or of little importance.

A coal <u>miner</u> does not have an easy job.
I have just one <u>minor</u> objection.
A ten-year-old is considered to be a <u>minor</u>.

MUSCLE/MUSSEL
Muscle is the flesh that moves a mammal's body; *mus-
sels* are shellfish like oysters.

It'll take a lot of <u>muscle</u> to lift that weight.
<u>Mussels</u> are a nice addition to clam chowder.

PAIR/PARE/PEAR
Pair means two; to *pare* is to cut or cut back; a *pear* is
a kind of fruit.

The <u>pair</u> of them looked very pleased.
We will have to <u>pare</u> our budget to the bone.
In October you can buy <u>pears</u> at the fruit store.

PAST/PASSED
Past is a noun; *passed* is a verb.

Stop living in the <u>past</u> or you will find that many of life's pleasures will have <u>passed</u> you by.

PEACE/PIECE
Peace is the absence of war or fighting, a *piece* is a part of.

After the war the combatants signed a <u>peace</u> treaty.
May I have a <u>piece</u> of that pie, please?

PERSONAL/PERSONNEL
Personal means relating to one's self; *personnel* is a collective noun for employees.

This is a very <u>personal</u> matter.
The company treats its <u>personnel</u> well.

PRINCIPAL/PRINCIPLE
Principal means first or most important; *principle* is a value or basic truth.

My <u>principal</u> reason is that I am basing my judgement on a set of <u>principles</u>.

RAIN/REIN/REIGN
Rain is water falling from the sky (noun); *reign* (verb or noun) is to rule; *rein in* is to restrain (verb).

I prefer <u>rain</u> to snow.
The rider had to <u>rein</u> in her horse.
The Queen has had a long <u>reign</u>.

STATIONARY/STATIONERY

To be *stationary* is to be still; *stationery* is writing paper.

> *He remained <u>stationary</u> at the crosswalk.*
> *You can buy good <u>stationery</u> at this bookshop.*

STRAIT/STRAIGHT

A *strait* (noun) is a narrow body of water between two larger ones; *(straight)* adjective is in a direct line.

> *The <u>Strait</u> of Georgia is off the coast of British Columbia.*
> *After the party they went <u>straight</u> home.*

THEIR/THEY'RE/THERE

Their is a possessive pronoun; *they're* the contraction of they are, and *there* is the opposite of "here".

> *Many people save <u>their</u> money to buy property.*
> *They think <u>they're</u> well off if they have no debts.*
> *<u>There</u> are others who just can't seem to save anything.*

TO/TOO/TWO

To is a preposition; *too* means also; *two* is a number 2.

> *It takes <u>two</u> <u>to</u> tango. It takes <u>two</u> <u>to</u> waltz <u>too</u>.*

WAIST/WASTE

Waste is to use up unnecessarily; the *waist* can be found near the middle of the body.

It seems a shame to <u>waste</u> such a large <u>waist</u> on one person.

WEATHER/WHETHER

Weather has to do with climate; *whether* means if it is true or probable that.

The <u>weather</u> is very unpredictable at this time of year.
I doubt <u>whether</u> we can do anything about it.

WHOLLY/HOLY

Wholly means completely; *holy* is being good in a religious sense.

I am <u>wholly</u> in agreement that Ghandi was a holy man.

WHOSE/WHO'S

Whose is a possessive pronoun; *who's* a contraction.

<u>Whose</u> keys are these? Could they belong to the one <u>who's</u> coming back through the door?

WOULD'VE/WOULD OF

The correct form is *would have*, which in speech is

contracted to *would've* – hence the incorrect written form *would of*..

YOUR/YOU'RE

Your is a possessive pronoun; *you're* a contraction for *you are*.

> *Your conscience is what you're going to have to listen to.*

EXERCISES TO DO WITH YOUR CHILD

1. Punctuate the following paragraph:

Zak was flying through space not flying a plane or a starship just flying he was wheeling and spinning through blackness studded with spinning swirling points of light he flashed past planets dodged between asteroid belts smashed through meteor storms he had to keep moving because something was after him several somethings in fact a terrified glance over his shoulder showed zak his pursuers were still there a swarm of burning eyed jagged toothed monsters with long fiery tails of comets

From *Cyberspace Adventure* by Terrance Dicks

2. Insert quotation marks in this paragraph:

Dad, said Henrietta one sunny Saturday morning. What do you think I should do when I grow up?

Leave home, muttered her father from behind the newspaper.

From *Henrietta's Night Out* by Stan Cullimore

3. Spot and correct the following misspelt words:

When the allarm went off Nicky and Tasha sat up in there beds and staired. Mum wassn't their, but the cassette-player was on the floor by Little Joe's cot. On top of it was a note. 'Press Plae' said the note.

So Nicky slid out of bed and presed 'Play'. They wached as the tape in side started too go round and round, and out cam they're mother's cheerful ealy morning voice.

"Wakey-wakey!"

"Creepie!" said Nicky.

From *Press Play* by Anne Fine

4. Insert apostrophes in the following paragraph:

Soon after Christmas Im going to be fifteen years old. Youd never know it if you talked to Mum and Dad. Weve just had a big row about the party. Theyll only let me have one if its properly super-vised. Maybe theyll let us play musical chairs and pass the parcel. (Thats after theyve frisked every-one for drink on the way in, of course.)

From *Not Dressed Like That, You Don't!* by Yvonne Coppard

5. Can you list ten words beginning with "s"? (alliteration)

6. Put the correct their/there/they're in the following sentence:

_____ are sometimes different ways of spelling words which sound the same, but _____ meanings are different. _____ called homophones and _____ often hard to remember.

7. Eliminate all the unnecessary prose from this sentence:

The magnificent, soft-hued orange and pink sunset cast a warm pinky glow over the sun-dappled garden where the beautiful young bronzed lovers gazed with youthful longing, staring into the blue green of each other's eyes.

"You are so very unique," he whispered quietly to her. "There isn't no one like you".